A Man's Guide To Surviving Divorce

How To Cope & Move On With Life

by R.L. Blackwood

VAMPA MEDIA PRODUCTIONS

All such attributed photographs are subject to the copyright claims of each respective owner.

Legal Disclaimer

This publication provides information about divorce and includes references to certain legal and accounting principles. Although the author and the publisher believe that the included information is accurate and useful, nothing contained in this publication can be considered professional advice on any legal or accounting matter. You must consult a licensed attorney or accountant if you want professional advice that is appropriate to your particular situation.

"A Patient man has great understanding. A man who is quick to anger shows only folly."

Proverbs 14:29

Introduction

I work as a bartender and I wrote this book in my spare time, after my divorce was final. I am not going to go into specific detail concerning my divorce. It should suffice you to know that my divorce had it all. Infidelity, pregnancy, debts, property disputes, incompetent lawyers, thoughts of suicide, misery, pain, loneliness, isolation, help, healing and redemption.

I walked a painful lonely path for a long time to get through my divorce. I worked hard at healing and forgiving and trying to put my life back together. Candidly, I feel that I did a pretty good job. I had a lot of help and I still bear a lot of scars. However, I am here, alive, I can still look myself in the eye in the mirror and I have lost neither respect for myself or the ability to love another person. I call this my victory.

An odd thing happened to me the night before my final divorce hearing. I was working and a lone man was hanging around the bar all night. He talked to some people, drank, kept busy with games, etc. Finally, towards closing, when it was just him and I, he sat down at the bar. At times a bartender is expected to chat with the guests to break the silence. This was one of those times.

I started chatting. Idly at first, like the kind of conversation you would engage the cashier at the grocery store in. Nothing special at all. Then, for some reason, he decided to confide in me about his troubles. This happens a lot in a bar too. He told me about his divorce, how he was out of the house. He told me how he missed his kids and how he couldn't sleep.

I tell you now, that is was one of those odd moments in life when the hair on the back of your neck stands up, and you feel, for some reason, that you are exactly where you are supposed to be. I knew exactly what this man was going through. I had left my house and lived out of a suitcase. I had cried myself to sleep. I had stared at the ceiling in the wee hours of the morning praying to just pass out for a few hours. I had been tortured by the idea of my wife in the arms of another man. I knew the hell that this man was in. I couldn't help myself and I broke my rule, I started talking personally with the man.

I told him about what I had gone through. I told him tips that had helped me get to sleep at night. I told him where I had bunked up when I couldn't stand to be alone in my big empty house. I poured it out for him, open and honestly, in the hopes that he would feel that he wasn't alone.

He asked me lots of questions and told me things that I thought only I had thought in my head many months before. I could see that he was walking the same miserable path that I had walked. We talked until after closing and in the end we shook hands. For me, it was a good night. I felt that I had gotten up and made a little, tiny difference in another man's life. It felt good.

I turned it over in my head for a few days, and I couldn't shake the feeling that there was more I could do. I had helped this man, but I wanted to help others too. No one should have to live alone at night trying to come up with reasons to not kill themselves. No one should have to feel, at the same time, that they are the only ones who are or have or will go through the hell of a divorce. I also, wanted to breathe a little bit of hope from the end of the divorce process into the lives of those at the beginning of it. I have lived it from beginning to end. While I am not an expert, I certainly feel that I have a few pearls of gritty wisdom to pass on.

That's why I wrote this book. This is my attempt at getting my voice, my experience and maybe my hope out to all those poor men that are suffering through the agony that is a divorce crisis. I sincerely hope that this helps you in some way. I am so sorry that you find yourself where you do. All I can say is that I got through it with scars. I got through it and you can too. If, you do the work to heal, you too will survive.

I would like to note here that this book is directed towards a male audience. I would like to say that through my divorce, I did not adopt any hating of women. Far to the contrary, many of the people that helped me the most in this process were women and I have a great love for many of them. The reason that I chose to write this book from a man's point of view, is simply because I am a man. Honestly, I do not feel confident that I could capture divorce from a woman's point of view in order to do it justice. So, I shrank from the challenge. I hope you will not think less of me for my reluctance.

This is not to say that this book cannot be helpful to women. On the contrary, indeed it may be very helpful. Just know up front that the bias is towards a male audience.

Well, that is all I have for this introduction. I would like to thank that anonymous man for inspiring this work. I never did hear how things ended up, but I sincerely hope for the best.

R.L. Blackwood

<u>Chapter 1</u>
Triage

When a person first shows up at the emergency room after having undergone some kind of a trauma, medical professionals perform what is known as triage.

Triage is a type of analysis that helps doctors figure out which problems requires the most immediate attention. For example, if a man is brought in suffering from a heart attack and cancer, the doctors are going to work to solve the heart attack problem first. Both problems can be fatal in the long run, but cancer will kill slowly, a heart attack can kill you in a few minutes.

When you are suffering through a divorce crisis, you are experiencing a very real trauma and applying triage can help. Your most immediate concern, just like doctors, is to stabilize the situation. In the case of a divorce, "the situation" is your life and your emotional state.

This needs to be your first goal in surviving your crisis and beginning to heal. You need to "stabilize" your life enough that dealing with the rest of the challenges that lay ahead of you will not overwhelm you.

This chapter is going to present you with several ideas that were amazingly beneficial to me, during my crisis. Some of these ideas and concepts may seem preachy, cliche or downright silly. A few of them did to me when I was in the beginning phases of my divorce crisis. However, I kept them in my mind, and continued to consider and reflect on them, and in time all of them came to be of use to me in stabilizing my emotional state and my life enough to be able to tackle the other obstacles that lay in front of me. I present them now, in the hopes that they may be of similar help to you.

Defining A Divorce Crisis

A divorce crisis, for the purposes of this book, is the time that your marriage first begins to suffer a threat that it will break up all the way through the final divorce hearing and even beyond. When it is over is really a personal decision.

I want to state now, so there is no confusion, that I am always against a marriage ending in divorce. It is a sad tragic thing. You should always look towards a divorce as a last resort. The scars that a divorce leaves can be very hard to heal.

You should, with a trusted counselor, always work towards communication, openness, understanding, acceptance, forgiveness and reconciliation if possible. However, sometimes, it just isn't in the cards. The rest of this book is written for those whom reconciliation has failed.

If you are, or fear you are going to become on of the unlucky ones, please read on. A painful road lies ahead of you, but it is my sincere belief that this book can help you on that journey.

"I Have Faith That Things Will Work Out"

This is one of those sections that might sound a little cliche, but it is, in my opinion, the most important section in this book and one you cannot forget.

No matter where you are in your divorce crisis, you need to accept and reinforce in your mind that things are going to be alright. You need to create and nourish a faith in this concept. This may seem impossible to you at the moment. I know it did to me when I was first told this idea. I even laughed through my tears. However, I really had hit rock bottom and decided I had nothing to lose.

I didn't believe it at first, but I wanted to. I wanted to very badly. So, what I did was I repeated the header of this section to myself. I did this constantly. I did it when I started being overwhelmed with emotion at work or when I was lying in my bed falling asleep alone. I did this when I felt sad and empty. I just kept repeating it to myself. It was my mantra. Sometimes, when my mind would spin and I couldn't fall asleep, I would just keep repeating it to myself as some kind of mental white noise that drowned everything out. Eventually I would fall asleep.

You might not believe that things will work out alright. There may be terribly painful and challenging moments ahead, but you will find that as time passes, life will improve gradually as time heals the wounds you have suffered. Life will find a new normal. As you continue to repeat this mantra to yourself, in faith, eventually you will begin to see the truth of it, in the improving situation of your life. Give it a try. You will not be sorry you did, and it will be the first step you take toward healing.

Your Life Isn't Over

When my wife first told me that she wanted a divorce, I went out of my mind. I felt like my whole world was crashing in and everything was over. I was a failure and would never amount to anything. Essentially, I felt about as bad about myself as I possibly could. I was drowning in self pity with occasional thoughts of suicide. It was not a good place.

No one ever wants to find themselves in a place like that. This is a fear that we all share. However, I have found that life has a funny way of working itself out. Finding yourself in a dark place is really just an opportunity to start walking towards the light.

Now, that last bit may sound a little preachy. I won't say that it isn't. But preachy is often what you need when you are first facing a divorce. The fact that it's true is important as well.

When we hit rock bottom, and realize that we may have made some big mistakes and are faced with misfortunes, we are in a very special place. We have the opportunity to look at our lives without the rose colored glasses. We can see who we really are and what we are really made from. This gives us the opportunity to improve ourselves and to grow as people.

This is a painful, but immeasurably rewarding experience.

You may feel like you life is over now. However, it is not. I feel, as painful as my divorce was, that I grew as a person from it. I emerged on the other side with perspectives and appreciations that I never would have found without it. Lastly, as odd as it may sound, I am happier now that I have ever been. Without my divorce, that too would have been impossible.

Each Day It Will Get A Little Better

In the very early days of my divorce, I did a lot of swinging between misery and rage. I was hurt and I was angry that I had been hurt. I was an emotional wreck and my heart was swinging between two very negative extremes. I would never have believed the title of this section if someone had told me. You probably don't if you are reading it now.

Well, in the end, it wouldn't have mattered if I had believed it then. I know it now. You will too. In the end, the pain subsides, the divorce concludes or the marriage reconciles and you are left with the chance to rebuild your life. In some cases, it can be better than it ever was before. Trust me. Tell yourself this everyday, whenever it gets hard and just keep going. Have faith in this fact. You will see it for yourself soon enough if you just keep going.

Thoughts Of Suicide

If a man is shot and the gut and dies from the wound, no one is surprised. The same can be said from any number of physical injuries. These injuries, as well, if not properly cared for can leave a man crippled for life.

The same can most definitely come from the emotional wounds caused by divorce and infidelity. I know men who are still crippled from their divorce. They look physically able and the walk around but they have never been able to heal emotionally and they may have even lost the ability to love. They are hobbled indeed.

I am not one of these, but the emotional wounds I received led me to the point that I was sitting at my desk with a loaded pistol in my hand considering whether or not to end my life. I was very close to death indeed and I stayed there for a long time, just thinking, trying to decide to live or die. I'm not proud of them moment, and I have only myself to blame, but I will certainly not pretend that it did not happen nor that the emotional wounds I had received almost ended my life.

Thoughts of suicide are very common in a divorce. They would creep up on me for a long time in the long, dark alone hours of the night. I fought them off every time, but I did live in fear of the time I would be too tired to do so. I did take a number of steps to help me just in case.

First, I slept with a phone next to the bed and I had programmed the number of two suicide hotlines into my phone. Just in case one was busy, I thought a back up would help. Fortunately, these numbers are not hard to find. In my area, one is offered by the county. One was also offered through my EAP (to be discussed later).

Secondly, as I am a gun owner, I got all of my guns out of the house. There were still plenty of things that I could have used to hurt myself, but at least I deprived myself of the convenience of a gun.

Thirdly, I recognized that thoughts of suicide were a medical emergency indeed. After the first time with a gun, I vowed that before I ever got to that point again, I would go to the emergency room of my local hospital. I even drove there once just to make sure I knew the way. I never used this option, but I did prepare myself that I may have to one day.

Emergency room workers will consider thoughts of suicide to be a medical emergency too. It is a legitimate mental health emergency. Don't ever be afraid to go to an emergency room if you get to this point. You cannot be too careful in your emotional state. Trained medical professionals will help you in an ER. It could save your life.

By helping to prepare for these feelings, and giving myself an outlet to help vent them, I am alive to today and I am happy. Now that you are facing a divorce, it would be wise of you admit that these feelings may exist and preparing for any storms that may develop.

Admit You Are In Trouble

I tossed and turned in my empty wedding bed for quite a few weeks when my divorce started. I drifted in and out of desperate sleep just long enough to be haunted by nightmares, to wake up confused as to why the bed was empty.

That was one of the worst parts, I would wake up, find the bed empty and be confused, forgetting all that had happened. Only then, in a cruel twist of fate would I come to my senses enough to remember that my wife was gone, and was sleeping in the bed of another man.

I would then get up and wander the house, clean, ride my bike at all hours on deserted city streets without a helmet or light. This went on for a while.

One night, I was riding my bike and I thought of a divorced man I know. His life fell apart when he divorced and he has never recovered. He lives his life everyday thinking of and still drowning in the pain of the divorce. He never dealt with it and it haunts him to this day. At that point, I broke down and found myself crying on the side of a deserted suburb sidewalk at 4 in the morning or so. But inside, I had resolved to do everything in my power to avoid becoming this man.

I admitted to myself then and there that I was in trouble. If you are going to survive your divorce and avoid becoming a man like the one that I know, you need to do this too. You need to look into yourself and find the courage to admit that you are in trouble and that everything is not OK. This can be hard. I did it and you can too. Once you have done this, you have taken the first step towards healing.

Admit That You Need Help

The first thing you need to do when you are staring down the barrel of a divorce is to admit that you are in an emotional crisis and your life and mental state have been turned upside down and thrown into turmoil.

I was definitely full of conflicting emotions that changed on a daily basis. I was hurt more than I ever had been in my life. I had a kaleidoscope of fantasies that changed with my mood, the time of day and whatever else was going on in my world. One minute I would be drowning in rage and revenge fantasies, the next day I was dreaming of a reconciliation with my wife. I was a messed up wreck and was in no position to make rational educated decisions.

When your life takes a nosedive towards the toilet, its funny what you think of. In my case, what came to mind was Franklin D. Roosevelt's brain trust. That seemed like a good idea in one of my moments of clarity.

I resolved that I was going to need to assemble a team of people whose services I needed to get through this. In my case, I got up the next day and made appointments to see an attorney, a counselor, a priest and a medical doctor.

You too, are going to need help. Just accept this. Going it alone is not a good idea. Even if you are a man who is used to going it alone, admit that you need help now.

Get Comfortable Thinking About Yourself

In triage, a medical responder assess the emergency situation and makes some hard choices. In some cases, they must decide that someone is beyond help. In the case of military medics, they are trained to make the decision that someone is beyond helping and to focus their resources on the person that can be saved. This is a painful and difficult decision and bears a striking resemblance to the decision you must make.

As a man who loves his wife, you are accustomed to caring for her and looking out for her interests and well being as much as you are your own. I was certainly this way. However, when you are confronted with a divorce crisis, you have to make the decision to step back and allow your wife to do what she will, while you focus on taking care of yourself and your children.

This was probably the hardest decision I made during the initial phase of my divorce crisis. I had tried for months to reach out to my wife. I had talked to friends and family trying to find some common ground. At times, I feel, I worried more about her than I did myself, as I was grappling with depression, loneliness and even thoughts of suicide. I was in a very dangerous place and all I could think about was trying to help her. I was making the wrong decision. Admitting that was one of the hardest decisions I have had to make in my life.

I remember making that decision well, however. I was sitting in our bedroom and was looking at all the pictures of our life on the walls. It had been a very rough and lonely day. Nothing special jarred the conclusion free, but I remember it clearly. I realized that I needed to take care of myself and my family. No matter what may come down the road, I needed to take care of me first. I needed to heal, before I could help anyone else to do so.

I likened the whole situation to two people in a car accident. The first thing you do when you are in a fender bender is to make sure that you are alright. That, indeed, everything is where it is supposed to be. Then and only then do you get out of the car to make sure that the other person is OK. What I realized that day, was that I was not OK, and that I needed to get myself right before I could see about helping anyone else. This whole line of thought runs contrary to what a good man might think and it definitely is not the kind of philosophy that they teach in kindergarten. However, it is sound thinking that will help you to get through this divorce and onto the road that leads to healing.

Being Wary Of Drugs and Alcohol

I have never had a problem with either drugs or alcohol. However, I feel that I should include a few words discussing drug and alcohol abuse in this work for completeness. A lot of the people that I have spoken with, while they were working through their divorces, had struggles with these substances. I have to admit that I was tempted to use them to mentally check out of my situation as well.

I am not telling you to stop having a beer with friends after work. I am also not telling you to never take a prescription medication to help you fall asleep. Both of these are fine. What I am telling you that you need to be wary of is increased consumption and dependence on alcohol and drugs as a means to cope with your divorce. If you are using drugs and alcohol to check out of your life, or to regulate your mood, you may have a problem. You should be watchful for:

- Increased consumption
- Drinking or taking drugs alone
- Drinking/ taking drugs to fall asleep
- Drinking or taking drugs to feel normal
- Drinking or taking drugs to avoid facing reality
- Drinking or taking drugs before or during work

This is really just a short list of activities that can indicate you are beginning to rely on substances to manage and cope with your emotions. This is where trouble usually begins.

This is an especially sensitive subject if you have a past history or substance abuse. If this is the case, I would recommend that you discuss ways to pre-empt a relapse with your counselor or family support network before it becomes an issue. You need to have a plan before you make your situation worse by turning to drugs and alcohol again. Get to a meeting, talk to your sponsor, counselor or family. Just get a plan together quickly before you lose control.

This Is An Emergency – Act Accordingly

You need to understand that a divorce is one of the most painful emotional experiences that you will face in your life. It is not a joke or an exaggeration to say that a divorce is an emotional strain that is on par with the death of a parent. In my divorce, there were many moments, when I sincerely believed it would have been easier if my wife had died. Of course, I do not mean that I wished or wished her any harm, I just thought the emotional burden would have been less.

When a loved one dies, no one questions that their life is facing an emergency. People tend to flock to your side and offer you sympathy. The sufferer seems to have much less trouble accepting that it is an emergency. This is not the case with a divorce. A lot of people try to put on a brave face and carry on like everything is fine. If they did this after their spouse had died, their friends and family would be worried, however, during a divorce it is not only tolerated, but sometimes encouraged.

You are facing an emergency in your life and you need to act accordingly. This is what savings are for, this is what personal time at work is for, this is what friends and family are for. This is when you need the help of doctors, counselors, clergy and attorneys. Do not bury your grief. Admit that it is there and admit this is a real emergency. Instead, draw on your sources of strength to carry on.

Don't Make An Ass Of Yourself & Grovel

A lot of men when faced with divorce, go into a silly panic mode. I know that I did. I made a bit of a fool of myself buying flowers and cleaning the house. I was under some desperate assumption that if I did these little things my wife would be convinced of my love for her and everything would be fine. I am sure that I reeked of desperation the whole time I was scrubbing the floor.

Do yourself a favor and avoid this step if you can. Don't feel bad if you fall down and wind up going through this stage. One thought might help you. You may still be able to save your marriage, but women have difficulty loving men that they do not respect. Groveling and putting on silly jackass displays of affection do not make women respect you and they will only hurt your cause here.

If you feel that you need some space to prevent yourself from doing these things do so. Get out of the house for a bit and check into a motel or a short term apartment.

Whatever you do, avoid:

- sending flowers
- late night calls
- drunk dialing or texting
- any kind of grand romantic gesture

Whatever happens in your divorce, you don't want to sacrifice your self respect getting there. If you have made mistakes own up to them like a man, but don't bend over backwards in a futile attempt to instantly re-kindle lost love. That may come, but later down the road. A band aid like flowers is not going to fix all of this.

Don't Confront Anyone!

Infidelity was part of my divorce and at times, especially at night, the thought of it made my blood boil. I would drown in rage and sorrow all night. My mind would twist through violent fantasies of revenge that would make Hollywood horror movies look tame. I know what it is to be eaten up by rage, pain and misery. I really do.

However, if there is one piece of advice that I can offer you while you are coping through your divorce; it is to not give into these emotions and avoid any situation that would lead to a violent confrontation.

Honestly, if you are going through a divorce, your life sucks already. I'm sorry, but it's true. You do not need to know what the inside of a holding cell looks like, you don't need the added headache of civil lawsuits and restraining orders and your kids don't need to see their father arrested.

You need to avoid these at all costs. Now, this is easier said that done and preparing to avoid these is a perfect subject to bring up with your counselor. They can help you walk through specific scenarios and help you to plan your response to them. They can help you to develop your mantra and other tools to help calm you down and to think rationally.

However, that may not cover every situation. Sometimes events unwind in a way that we may not predict. This happened to me one morning and I almost lost control. I honestly felt like I was someone else and I came so close to doing things that I would regret now. The hair on the back of my neck stands up when I think of it now. I did the only thing that I still had control enough to do and I ran out of the house. I just ran away from it all. Literally.

I ran and ran until I didn't know where I was and I felt like my heart was going to explode. I finally had to call a friend to come get me because I was actually lost. If you ever find yourself in a situation like I did, just get out of there. Remove yourself from the situation and let things calm down. Run away if you have to. It may seem silly, but it kept me from doing something I would have really regretted, and possibly helped me avoid a jail term.

Playing Nice Is Cheaper, Better And Easier

I've already told you that I am not an attorney. I have no legal training at all. However, I do know that playing nice in a divorce is cheaper in the end.

You may want to hurt your wife by breaking something she cares about or by throwing out her shoe collection. It may offer you some peace, maybe even amusement and revenge, for a minute or two. However, in the end, childish acts like this really only nourish an antagonistic, self destructive cycle.

In the end, playing nice will make your divorce more bearable, cheaper and it will make everything end sooner. That is what you want. I promise you. Any petty victory you get by flushing her pet goldfish down the toilet will pale in comparison to a cheap, uncomplicated, quick divorce. Keep your eyes on that prize and let the pettiness fall by the wayside. You're an adult. Act like one.

Be Careful About Digging

One of the most frustrating aspects of my own divorce was the lack of information. I did not know what had brought this on. At times, I didn't even know where my wife was living. I was in the dark.

Now, I am naturally an inquisitive person, and I wanted to understand the full scope of what was happening. To me, this was necessary before I could react. I didn't want to make a wrong decision based on bad information. So I went digging.

I am not proud of what I did, but my counselor has told me that it is fairly normal. I dug a lot. I looked through journals and read emails. I looked for anything and everything that could help explain to me where this so unexpected storm had come from. I found answers.

However, many of the answers that I found were painful for me to see. I will not get into the full details of course. That is not necessary, and I want to stay on topic. Suffice to say, that I wish I had not seen many of them. There is no taking any of it back now. What they say is really true, ignorance is bliss.

I have hopefully, at this point, empowered you a bit. It is my sincere hope that you know that you alone can make decisions concerning how you conduct yourself during this crisis. You will need to decide for yourself if you go looking for answers to painful questions. However, before you decide to, just know that it would have been less painful for me if I had chosen not to.

This Is A Process...It Takes Time

A divorce is a complicated, messy affair no matter how amiable it is. There are lots of things to sort out like:

- Who get's the house?

- Who get's the car?
- Who's paying for our credit card debt?
- Who's paying the school loans?

This brief list doesn't even take into account children and the healing from the emotional trauma that you are going through. Add into this lawyer consultations on lunch periods and counseling on your days off and state mandated waiting periods and you get the idea that your divorce is going to take a lot of time and even more patience from you.

I found this one of the most frustrating aspects of my divorce. I waited six months before I started any kind of divorce proceedings in the hopes of reconciliation. However, once it became painfully clear that this was not an option, I wanted to be done with the whole affair as soon as possible. However, this wasn't possible.

I had to be patient and remind myself that this was a process, not a switch and I couldn't speed it up. This became another one of the mantras that I constantly reminded myself of. I was involved in a process and all the wishing in the world could not make it go faster than it was going to take. I had to accept it and I did. You will have to do this too.

I'm Sorry But You Can't Trust Your Wife

I worked with a couple of attorneys through my divorce. One day, I was meeting one of them in the coffee shop of a grocery store for a quick consultation. We talked a lot of numbers and strategies. In the end, I decided that this attorney wasn't a good fit for me. However, she did say one thing that caught my attention. She said that because my wife was asking for a divorce, she was focused on her self first. She added that because of this, I could not trust her any more.

At first this comment upset me. I had married my wife proudly on a tropical beach and I had always held her in high regard. I still wanted to rebuild a life with her. It left me with a bad taste in my mouth. However, I couldn't get the thought out of my head. I kept turning it over and it wouldn't go away. In the end, I was forced to look the ugly truth in the eye and accept that I couldn't trust my wife anymore. It was a painful sobering thought.

Unfortunately, if you are reading this book, you are most likely faced with a similar problem. Of course, you will need to decide what to do with your life, this is after all, your path. However, be careful about issuing trust. Don't let your emotions blind you to reality. Trust is based on repeated behaviors over time. You trust that the sun will come up everyday or that hot coffee will burn you. When you married your wife, you and her both pledged to cherish one another forever. Now that a divorce crisis is looming, sadly, you cannot be certain of her intentions, and you need to protect yourself. An old bit of advice is very relevant here. Hope for the best, but prepare for the worst.

Sex & Dating Are For After Your Divorce

Sex is a difficult subject to tackle at times, but sex is one of the first things I thought of when I was hit with my divorce. I had been married for years and been in a long term committed monogamous relationship for even longer. Candidly, I was used to frequent love-making and I quickly noticed its absence.

It wasn't just the physical sensation of release that I was missing. It was all those little intangibles that making love to a woman offers. I missed the way her skin felt, the way her hair smelled or the feel of another heartbeat in an embrace. I missed it all.

When my divorce first started I considered pursuing other women in my life and I even considered hiring prostitutes. The last one was actually the most appealing of all the ideas I had come up with for satisfying my needs. There were no strings attached and no one would ever have to know.

The idea of starting to date another woman was even more perilous. My life had been torn up, my emotions were raw and I was still having all kinds of fantasies of avenging my broken heart. I realized that in a situation like this, again, I could not trust my emotions and I could very easily find myself with confused feelings of love for both my new girlfriend and my wife.

All these confused feeling made me far too vulnerable and emotionally unprepared for sex. I laughed when I realized that I was in the exact position a fourteen year old boy finds himself. I was horny as hell, but my emotions were no where near ready to engage in healthy sex as much as I just wanted to get laid.

I made a resolve then and there to wait six months before I engaged in any sort of adult/sexual activity. It may seem short for you, but to a horny man it will seem like forever! It sure felt like that to me. But, I still think this is one of the best decisions I made during my divorce.

The decision gave me the ability to let my emotions calm down and allowed me to begin to trust my decisions again. You should consider similar restrain. A Russian Czar once famously quipped "One rarely regrets having waited". He might have had a point.

Be Careful About Irreversible Decisions

When you are first confronted with a divorce, usually, you will go into panic mode. This is what I did for sure. I would say that the first month of my divorce is nothing short of hazy. It's a lot like a bad dream that I have trouble remembering. This is not the time to make irreversible decisions.

I will tell you that I made some decisions that I will have to live with for the rest of my life. In my case, I had some tattoo work done. Now, I didn't do anything stupid like tattoo my wife's name on my chest. However, the tattoos I did get are forever. Now, in my case, this is not something that upsets me. However, in retrospect, this was not the best time to be making permanent decisions.

This word of caution applies to many different decisions. Tattoos are just on example. Be careful about:

- Tattoos
- Vasectomies
- Selling or giving away property
- The words that you say. What happens if you later want to reconcile?
- How you treat your children, family and friends. Memories last forever too.

I am not trying to tell you how to run your life. However, I am warning you that, in the middle of a divorce, is not the time to be making permanent decisions. Just be aware of this. Your awareness will help you to identify these situations, step back, and postpone them for a later, calmer time.

You Get More Than One Chance At Love

When I first started my divorce experience, one of the things that kept me up at night was a fear that I had blown my one chance at love and happiness. This wasn't a rational fear. Honestly, this was the kind of irrational fear that plagues a mind at night when it cannot sleep.

I am just going to say this here for your sake. Let me assure you that there is more than one person that can make you happy. We get more than one chance at love in life. I have loved since my divorce and I am certain that you can too. Don't loose faith!

Steel Is Made In Fire

One thing that you should consider in this triage part of the book is that you will emerge stronger and usually better from this ordeal if you work through the process and focus on healing yourself.

A benefit that not a lot of people see is that having been through the horrors of a divorce, this can make you more resilient in your relationships and less fearful of loss. You have been through it, so you know what it is like. You survived one, you can do it again.

A lot of people also emerge with a greater sense of themselves. I sincerely feel that this was both one of the greatest pains in my life, but also the greatest opportunity to learn who I am, that I am a decent man and that I can rebuild my life. I know it sounds weird, but I honestly believe I benefited a great deal from the ordeal and know myself much better as a person because of it.

The path you are walking is filled with peril, but don't lose sight of the opportunities to learn and grow and the subtle rewards that may line the trail. It is just possible, that like steel, you will emerge stronger from this fire.

Divorced Men Are In High Demand

For me, one of the biggest concerns during my divorce, was how I would go about meeting another woman and dating again. I had been out of the dating game for a long time and I didn't have any confidence in my ability to jump back into the pool. Well, I can tell you, that is a worry, I was silly to spend any time on. Let me tell you, divorced me are in high, high demand. In fact, you will quickly become a highly sought, eligible bachelor.

At first, this fact puzzled me. It seemed that a man who was cast off by another woman would have trouble in the dating scene. Well, that just isn't true at all. As a bartender I have the opportunity to meet and talk with lots of women. (This is not how I date. Never get your meat where you get your bread.) Through quite a few conversations, they were kind enough to open my eyes.

Here is how it was explained to me. First, more women are born than men. This means that from the beginning, there are not enough men to go around. As a result, more women wind up single into their thirties and forties. This means there are even fewer men to go around. Men also die at a higher rate. This only further serves to diminish the pool of eligible gentlemen. Then of course a certain number are gay. Smaller still. Then, of the single men that remain in their thirties and forties, a lot of them are not interested in commitment. If they haven't married by, say 35, they are often viewed as flawed. Smaller still.

Then you come along. A straight man, who is willing to commit, has a good heart, a stable life, who may have just married the wrong woman, but who still has a lot to offer. To a single woman in her thirties and up, you are gold! You are just what they are looking for. I have known women who have told me that their next boyfriend will be some nice divorced man! They are actually out there looking for you.

Now, this is all based on hearsay and empirical evidence, but you should trust me. Divorced men make very eligible bachelors. This gave me a lot of hope and comfort and I hope it will do the same for you. No matter what happens.

Chapter 2
First Aid

Continuing with the medical emergency theme that I started in Chapter 1, after triage comes first aid. The patient has been stabilized. They're still in bad shape and all those injuries that they have sustained need to be addressed. We need to stitch, bandage, etc. etc.

You are in the same position. There are a lot of minor details that you need to attend. You need to find professionals to help you. You need to contact banks and insurance companies. You need to make sure things you care about are safe. At the risk of mixing metaphors, the storm is coming and you need to make sure everything is in order so you can weather it as comfortably and with as little damage as possible.

That is what this chapter is about. This chapter will walk you through a detailed list of steps that you can take to make sure that you are as well prepared as you can be for the coming storm. I went through all of these steps in my divorce, and I like to think that they made the process of the divorce simpler and smoother. This meant that many technical details were taken care of in the beginning and I could focus on healing my emotional wounds instead. Let's get started.

This Is Going To Take A Lot Work

Thomas Paine once said, "That which we gain to easily, we esteem to lightly." There is a lot of truth in that old saying. I took it very much to heart in working through my divorce crisis. What I wanted was to build a new life and to find happiness for myself again.

However, there was a lot of work that needed to be done and it was not going to be easy.

I was going to need to work through the pain and emotional baggage that comes with any divorce. I was going to need to settle all the property, debt and money issues that come with a painful and messy separation. Lastly, I was going to need to deal with all the bureaucracy and tedium that comes with the legal aspect of divorce.

I enjoy my leisure time and I hate to work more than I have to. I like to enjoy my life. However, here I found myself in the depths of a huge hole and I needed to dig out. You too are going to need to get comfortable with the fact that cleaning up this mess is going to take a lot of work and patience on your part. However, you can get through it. I did and you can too.

Patience Is Your New Mantra

It is entirely possible that you will have the world's quickest, simplest and most cordial divorce. However, the odds suggest that your divorce, like so many others, will take a lot of time, and there will be many wrinkles to work out. This is true even in divorces where both parties are in complete agreement and there are no children to complicate matters.

This stuff just takes time. Accept that right now. You need to be patient and accept that it will take however long it will take. Refinancing can take forever. Many states impose waiting periods on divorces to make sure you really want this. Attorneys reschedule. Life happens. Accept it.

This can be maddeningly frustrating. Many times I just wanted it all to be over and behind me. That was all I wanted in the world. But, I had to keep waiting. Day by day I got closer as the conclusion seemed to draw ever farther away. However, in the end I got there and you will too, but you have to remain patient.

Building A Brain Trust

One of your first goals after you have calmed down and the shock has worn off a bit is to build yourself a brain trust. A brain trust is a group of experts and aides who can help you to think through the decisions that you are going to need to make in the future. You're going to need help.

There are two reasons that you need to construct a brain trust. The first of these is that many of the subjects that you are going to need to work (the law, psychology, medicine and God) are subjects in which an expert can help you. There may be technical matters and specifics about your situation that the Internet and this book just don't have the answers to. These people can help.

The second reasons that you want to construct a brain trust is that you may not be in the right state of mind to make complex, irreparable decisions on your own. You are going to need to have some people around you who are intimately acquainted with your situation who can tell you whether or not your thinking is sound. I did this a lot with my counselor. I would tell him how I was feeling or thinking or discuss a decision I had made. Then, I would look at him and say "Is that crazy?". A lot of the time I just needed someone dispassionate enough to tell me that what I was doing was OK, normal and sane.

These people will be your divorce team. With your help you can get through this divorce and move on with your life.

Attorneys

Divorce is a horrible, emotional process that tears families apart. It tore mine apart and broke my heart in the process. I felt at times that I would never be happy again and that life wasn't worth living.

However, in the midst of all that pain an heartache, I realized that marriage and divorce are not matters of the heart alone. The state and courts have a large part to play in the sad affair of the end of a marriage.

When my heart was first breaking, I didn't care a bit about money, property or my rights. I would have given up everything I owned in the vain attempt to fix my marriage and to try and re-win the heart of my wife.

Before I did, though, I went and talked to an attorney and you should do this as soon as possible in a divorce, even if you still hope to reconcile your marriage. Attorneys are very useful in making plain the dangers and perils you face and they can advise you on your options under the law better than anyone else can.

In my case, I was terrified that if my wife found out I was going to a divorce attorney it would only bring about the inevitable. I went and consulted with an attorney and paid cash so there was no trace of my act in the credit card bills or bank statements. I also entered the number of the attorney in my phone under a false name. In my case I used the name "Pizza".

It was really hard going to the attorney and hearing them tell me my options and to talk coldly about the death of my marriage, but it was also totally worth it. They spelled out my options well and gave me quite a few bits of advice that I put to good use. They were especially helpful in helping me figure out where I was going to live and what rights I would have if I did move out.

If you have never had the need of a divorce attorney, you may not know where to look. There are a few options that I would recommend.

First, if you have ever used an attorney in business or for another business like a will or trust, ask them for a recommendation for a divorce attorney in your area. Divorce law is a specialty, so they will most likely not be able to help you directly, but lawyers are a tight knit bunch and they will know at least some divorce attorneys in town.

If you have never used an attorney at all consider asking friends and family for their recommendations of competent attorneys. If the attorney is not a divorce attorney that they have used, but is someone they trust and recommend, they will be able to recommend someone.

The last place to look for an attorney is through your state's bar association. Each state maintains a bar association that is responsible for the licensing of all attorneys in the state. These bar associations will also provide lists of local attorneys that can help in specific matters. You will also be certain of their qualifications and competency.

Attorneys are like shoes and none are guaranteed to be a perfect fit for your situation. Visit an attorney and if you like them you can use them as your legal advisor. If you don't like them, don't be afraid to continue looking around. In this situation, you need an attorney that you will be comfortable with to support you. I went through two attorneys before I found legal representation that I really liked and stuck with.

Priests, Pastors, Rabbis or Imams

The idea of talking to a doctor, a lawyer and a counselor were all simple ideas to come to. These are very common people to talk with during a divorce. The idea of talking to a priest (I was raised Catholic) took longer.

What finally drove me to talk to a member of the clergy was the conclusion that the problems that I was struggling with existed in more dimensions than I had previously thought. I had spoken with an attorney to help protect my property, I had taken to a doctor to keep my body healthy and I had talked to a counselor to keep my mind from falling apart. However, I hadn't given any thought to my soul.

Actually, I had lived a very agnostic life for a long time. I couldn't remember the last time that I had gone to church voluntarily. Usually, it was just something I did around Christmas time and I couldn't wait for it to be over.

However, one night while I lay awake, I realized that the problem of a divorce and the heartbreak that comes with it, is one of those questions that religions exist to help us with. They offer comfort and solace to those to whom something tragic has happened. I recalled the old phrase "There are no atheists in foxholes.", and suddenly I understood exactly what that meant.

I first sought out a Catholic priest. Like I said, I had been raised Catholic, and it was easy to go back to my roots. This was several months into the crisis. I talked with a very kind priest, who did offer me comfort. In the long run, I did stop seeing him, in lieu of another pastor to whom I found that I had a better, more open connection. I actually comparison shopped members of the clergy.

However, realizing that the crisis in which I found myself had a spiritual dimension, was one of the most important parts of my healing process. It allowed me to begin to seriously cope with what had happened to me in an honest light.

In your own divorce crisis, I would strongly suggest that you set aside some time for yourself, and reflect on your situation in this light as well. I can't say that I profess one faith over another (I certainly don't endorse one) and would struggle which religion box to check on a survey. However, many religions deal with the simple truth that life is hard and help people to deal with this every day. You owe it to yourself to consider this resource and see how it fits into your own brain trust.

Counselors

In my professional life, I have recommended workplace employee assistance programs to people on many occasions. I know for a fact that few have ever taken me up on it, even when, I sincerely believe that they would have strongly benefited from counseling.

There seems to be some sort of aversion in people to the idea of counseling. Men and women seem to share this characteristic. I don't understand it. When I was first confronted with the fact that my marriage was crumbling, someone to talk to, who was objective was one of the first things I sought out. In fact, the first time I walked into a counselors office was less than 72 hours after the crisis started.

I cannot emphasize enough, how much I recommend going to a counselor. Talking with a counselor is immensely helpful and, as with all medical professionals, they are bound to maintain your privacy by law. You have nothing to lose!

If nothing else, setting up counseling appointments will give you an hour or so to unload your feelings to a completely partial, trained listener. This alone will make counseling worth it and is much better than simply keeping your feelings bottled up.

Finding a counselor is not hard and there are many resources available to you. You can ask for the recommendation of your doctor. This can help you find a counselor that is covered through your insurance network (counseling doesn't have to break the bank).

Additionally, many work places offer employee assistance programs (EAP) as part of their employee benefits package. Through one of these organizations, you can also find a provider in your area, again, that is compatible with your insurance. An added benefit of an EAP, is that sessions are usually provided absolutely free through a certain period of time. This can help with the triage part of your work. With no out of pocket cost, you really have nothing to lose and it can only help stabilize your life and emotional state.

Many cities and counties also have mental health crisis hotlines that can help refer you to a counselor. Remember, this doesn't mean you're crazy. Looking for help id one of the sanest steps you can take. Lastly, many clergy are trained as counselors as well. If you are part of a church community, this is a great resource to tap. We will talk more about churches when we talk about support groups.

As important as finding a counselor is to helping you through your divorce, finding a counselor that you are comfortable with is even more important. You need to be able to discuss very intimate and personal information with a counselor and you need to have faith that the person in whom you are confiding is right for you.

I went to two counselors while I was working through my divorce. There was nothing wrong with the first counselor, however, ultimately, I decided that I preferred going to a counselor with a religious background who was a family man. This was just a better fit for me. It was a hard decision, but it was for the best and I do not regret it at all. There is nothing wrong with talking to more than one counselor and shopping around. Often, they will have free consultations on a "get to know each other basis", these were very helpful to me in making my final selection. This also showed me that the counselor I chose was interested in helping me.

Remember, this is your journey and you need to find someone with whom you are comfortable speaking with, but you **DO** need to find someone.

Go To Your Doctor

One of the best decisions that I feel I made, when my divorce started, was to go to my doctor periodically. One of my fears was that I would be swept up in feelings of despair and depression and that this would cause other problems in my life. I was especially concerned with work and my friends.

I went to my doctor regularly, but not obsessively. I discussed how I was having trouble sleeping and my concerns about depression and anxiety. She was very helpful. She provided me with the documentation that I needed to get my insurance company pay for my counseling. Additionally, she provided me with sleeping pills and anti-anxiety pills in a controlled environment.

Your Family Support System

You may not be close with your family. I certainly was not when my divorce started, but they came to me and supported me through some of the darkest days of my life. The proved to me that blood is thicker than water.

You will need all the support that you can find to make it through this mess and heal. Your family can provide you with that. There is something special about the unconditional love of your family that makes their support all the stronger.

Sometimes reaching out to your family can be a huge challenge. I didn't tell them about the crisis and infidelity right away. I stewed and suffered for three days on my own. I actually told no one. I just swallowed everything. On the third night I couldn't take it anymore. I called and left a voice mail. All I said was something like "I'm in trouble." They came to me right away and were both amazingly supportive and helpful.

This is going to require sacrifice and openness on your part. Both of these were foreign to me and scared me a great deal. I found myself talking to my family about some of the most personal details of my life. At times this was uncomfortable and I felt bad about the burden that I was placing on them. Now I know that they were only too happy to help me carry it.

If you have family, I would recommend letting them into your life to support you, no matter how much you think you can do this on your own. They can provide invaluable support and comfort while you work to rebuild.

Lifelines & Crisis Hotlines

There were a few times during my divorce crisis where I found myself on the verge of panic. Sometimes, I had just been hit with some fresh emotional trauma, other times, my mind had spun out of control and the thought of the future was something I couldn't bear. These moments of panic were mostly confined to the first three months of the crisis, but they were very real.

They did quickly disappear, but I don't know how I would have coped if, early on in a moment of clarity, I had not setup some lifelines.

My lifelines were people that I could talk to when I found myself in a moment like this. I had a couple. The first was a close member of my family, the other was a very good friend, and the third was actually a mental health crisis line. All of them were great and very helpful, and between the three of them, there was always someone that I could talk to.

If I just needed someone to talk to, during the course of the day, I would call my friend or family member. They would usually talk to me for a few minutes, let me know everything would be ok, and that would be good. I just needed a pat on the head sometimes.

As much as I wanted to talk to them at four in the morning, I just couldn't bring myself to bother them. So, when I found myself needing to talk to someone at off hours, I would call the crisis hotline. This was definitely a great resource. The line was staffed with trained counselors, and they would just let me pour my heart out. It sounds weird now, but the phone and the anonymity made it easy. I would just unload my mind, free of charge, and they would listen. They would soothe, cope, and they were a huge help in getting me through the early, traumatic phase of my divorce.

Setting up and knowing who your lifelines are, **before you need them**, is something you should do right away. You can choose anyone you trust. Family and friends are your natural go to. However, if you don't have someone you feel comfortable with, then find the crisis hotlines in your area. Often these are run by churches, hospitals, the county, or in my case, my employee assistance program. Find these numbers and program them into your cell phone now. That way, they are ready whenever you need them. At this point, sadly, you never know when that will be.

Personal Legal Guidebooks – A Great Resource

Lawyers are expensive and going into a meeting with your attorney without any preparation is going to cost you hundreds of dollars in legal fees while he answers simple questions.

If you are reading this work, you are a bookish fellow and you are already looking for answers in your divorce. This is great. You are preparing by educating yourself on the subject of divorce. Keep that spirit up and go out and buy yourself a legal guidebook. You can find these in any bookstore or on any online retailer that sells books.

I strongly recommend getting one. In the long run these can be helpful in educating you on any legal situations from inheritance law to real estate questions. However, these always have a basic chapter on marriage and divorce law. This is usually referred to as "family law". Read this chapter twice. I mean it – twice. This will give you a very basic working knowledge of family law and it will give you the chance to speak intelligently and from an educated point of view

with your attorney. It will only make you better prepared for your divorce and it will make you more helpful to your attorney.

Own Your Decisions

A divorce is a highly personal experience. No one person's experience will be the same as anyone else's.
You need to know that from the beginning. I realized
this early on in my divorce, and I also realized that the
choices that I made then, were mine alone and would
affect me for the rest of my life.

Because the decisions that you make at this point are
so long lasting, and because of the fact that the experience is so personal, you need to define this path as
your own. You need to take control of those decisions.
You need to be the one to make them and you need to
own them when you do.

It would be a lot easier to let other people tell you what
to do. Trust me, they will try. Your friends will give
you advice. Your family will chime in. Your attorney
will tell you what to do. Your wife may even tell you
what to do. Listen and absorb, it's good to have other
perspectives, but you must be the one that makes the
final decision. Do what is best for you and your family.

Don't Let Friends And Peers Define This

When your friends and family first hear that you are in
the middle of a divorce crisis, their reactions may be-

come a little odd. From most people you would expect sympathy, however, too often their "support" may take on the feeling of anger.

I actually encountered a lot of this when my divorce started. People would pour out their souls to me and tell me about their own experiences with infidelity and divorce. I would listen and reflect on my own situation and I would hope to hear words of advice and wisdom that would be helpful. I didn't hear a lot of constructive ideas.

What I did hear a lot of were suggestions of violence and regrets about not having done so during their own crises.

Before long, I had a bit of an epiphany. What people were beginning to show to me since I was now a member of the "Divorce Club" were their own unsettled and tangled emotions concerning their own divorces. Many people don't process a divorce or break up in an analytical and emotionally healthy way and instead are left with regrets and bitterness. These feelings seem to well up when they feel they are with someone feeling the same way.

I recognized this, and I used this as an inspiration. I realized that many people that I had known for years still carried around unprocessed pain and anguish, as well as hurt and remorse and sorrow from their divorces. This is what happens when you bury pain and refused to do the work needed to heal.

I resolved that I would not become one of these people and that I would work my way through my divorce in a way that allowed me to heal, if only to still bear some scars.

I dismissed their hateful epithets that were directed at my wife and instead focused on the goal of my own healing. This was my journey and I had every intention that I would set the path that I was to follow towards new happiness.

Forgiveness & Healing Are The Goals

I was very conflicted in the beginning of my divorce as to what my goals should be. Should I focus on screwing my wife in court? Should I just leave the country and start a whole new life? Honestly, I didn't know what I needed to focus on.

It took me a long time, but I did figure out what the goal should be. It's a twin goal of healing and forgiveness. Now, when I type that, I will admit that it sounds a little wishy washy, but in all honesty it isn't. It is a completely self motivated act, that in the end helps others as well. Let me explain.

When faced with a crisis like the one you now face, you really stand at a fork in the road. You can only go one of two ways. You will either take the path that leaves you emotionally scarred and bitter from the experience, or you will take the path that will lead you to being a stronger individual who has healed and grown from the experience.

If you hang on to all the pain, hurt, and sadness that you feel now, you will inevitably wind up a bitter person. This will only cripple any future relationships on any level and will lead nowhere good. The only way that you (and your counselor) are going to be able to lay down the burden of the pain, hurt and sadness, is through the act of sincere forgiveness.

Depending on when you are reading this, you may not even believe that it is possible. Believe me, there was a time when I did not think so either. That is one of the reasons that I sought out a spiritual counselor for my brain trust. The act of forgiveness is a spiritual matter. It is hard work, and at times, I still struggle with it now, but I understand just how necessary it was and continues to be.

For your sake, and the sake of your future relationships and your emotional health, make forgiveness your goal. Only through this act, can you truly heal yourself and move on with your life a whole man.

EAPs

If you are like I was, and you have never sought or felt the need for counseling or help with a crisis in your life, you may not know where to turn. This is frustrating and and my emotional state was not one that allowed for patience. So I turned to my EAP and it was a great place to get started.

EAP stands for Employee Assistance Program and is a common benefit offered by companies these days. The idea is that an emotionally balanced and centered person makes for a better all-round employee. They are a great resource.

Most companies will hire a third party contractor to provide this service. You contact them and they connect you to the plan resources after a brief consultation. Generally there are so many free sessions, or the sessions are low fee. This all depends on your company's plan. To find out if your company has an EAP, contact your human resources department.

The first thing that I was worried about with an EAP is that my private information was going to somehow be funneled to my employer. Don't worry about this. Privacy laws exist to make sure that this does not happen. EAPs are restricted by the same confidentiality laws as doctors are.

I am a big fan of EAPs and I used my company's plan quite a bit initially (later I began seeing a counselor with more of a spiritual background). It was very easy to use and the feature that I found the most useful was they way that the EAP, through a crisis line was always available and connected me to local counselors trained to help me cope with my problems in a fast friendly manner. The first time I called the EAP and told them about my situation was a Friday night about

10 pm. They made it possible for me to be in the office of a licensed counselor at 11am the next morning.

Making A Good Faith Effort

This section may be a little controversial. However, I think I would be remiss if I did not write a bit about trying to reconcile with your wife.

I struggled with this quite a bit. When I first was confronted with divorce and infidelity, I was filled with negative emotions and the thought of ever trying to reconcile with my wife made my physically ill. Then I went and I talked with some of the brain trust I have described to you and a new bit of insight emerged. This was, that if I did not try to make a good faith effort to reconcile with my wife, there was a very good possibility that I would be plagued with doubts about how I had handled my divorce I would be left wondering if I could have saved things. I would have to live with this for the rest of my life. The certainty that I had tried, would (and does to this day) offer me closure and helped me to heal.

I swallowed my pride and looked past the infidelity, and tried to look at my wife as the woman I had fallen in love with, not the woman that had broken my heart. I called her and told her that I wanted us to go to counseling together. We did.

In the end, nothing changed and the divorce was finalized. However, the attempt offered me the closure that I was seeking.

As I wrote earlier, this is your journey and the path you walk is defined only by you. However, I would strongly recommend that you consider this. In Arabic, the words for truth and forgiveness are both names for God. This is a powerful message of how important these concepts are. Before you throw everything away, open your mind and see the truth that your wife has been an important person in your life and open your heart to the possibility of forgiving her.

I will not say that anything will work. It did not in my case, however, I do not for one second regret the decisions that I made to try and mend what we had. In the end, the decision is yours alone to make.

Setting Time Lines

Opening the door and working towards reconciliation, even if fruitless, will be helpful for your mental state and your conscience. You tried everything you could. I did exactly that. However, I added a time line to the equation that helped me to keep everything in perspective.

I made a deal with myself that I was going to put my life on hold for six months. I wasn't going to date anyone, engage in any sexual activity, or move ahead with the divorce formalities such as filing and refinancing the house in just my name.

The goal of this was twofold. First, it offered the chance at reconciliation time to develop. Emotions get clouded and run strong in the middle of a divorce. The pause offered a chance for those emotions to settle and their sincerity to be tested.

The second reason that I chose to do this was that it allowed my own emotions to settle out. Specifically, it helped my anger and hurt to subside so I could, with the help of my brain trust, make rational calm decisions. Panicked decisions are always decisions that should be questioned.

My goal during this time line was simply to reestablish a connection with my wife and to begin the healing process. At the end of the six months if we had still found ourselves in counseling, I would have chosen to extend the time line and continue working towards healing and reconciliation. In the end this did not happen. At the end of the six months nothing had changed and I made the decision to move ahead with my divorce.

Setting a time line and writing it on a calendar or putting the date in your cell phone will help to keep you on track. It will serve as a measurable milestone of progress and it will create a time when you can review progress or the lack thereof. In your divorce I would recommend that you set time lines to help keep yourself on track to either completing the divorce or rebuilding your marriage.

Divorce Is Expensive

I have always been a big fan of saving money and I hate credit cards. However, when I was first hit with my divorce, that drive began to weaken. I figured my life was over, I might as well just spend money to make me happy. I did this for a while, until finally, I realized how much a divorce can cost and just how much I had to lose.

A that point, I stopped my reckless spending and my investing and began hoarding as much cash as I could.

This is not to say that you cannot spend some money. I certainly spent a bit of money traveling and trying to keep sane, but you should also be conscious of how much you are spending and how much money you have in reserve. Divorces are expensive and you are going to need to spend a bit of money.

Forget lawyers, where I live, it costs $300 just to file your divorce papers with the county. That's a sobering thought indeed.

Pile Up Emergency Cash

Unfortunately, while marriage is about romance, divorce is about money, assets and business. This is the ugly flip side of marriage. As such, divorces tend to consume cash at an alarming rate. I'm sorry to have to break this to you.

This was certainly true in my divorce. I couldn't believe how quickly bills piled up. I was living in a furnished apartment, while I still paid the mortgage, so there were two households to support. Insurance co-pays, lawyers fees, court fees, and counseling costs all added up quickly and my once large emergency fund, dwindled. This was just another layer of stress to me. However, the even worse alternative would have been to have had to finance my divorce. Think about that. Actually paying interest for the privilege of having my world torn apart. That was something I just wouldn't do.

Well, I went on an austerity rampage to free up cash. I stopped everything that wasn't essential. I cut out 401k allocations, I canceled cable, and raised insurance deductibles. I sold investments (sometimes even at a loss) and stopped paying down debt (I did keep up minimums) to make sure that I had plenty of cash on hand to deal with all the bills. It wasn't easy but I don't regret one decision I made. Of all the problems that I faced through my divorce, I am proud to say that cash flow was not one of them.

These are the steps that I took to make sure my divorce was well funded. I am not saying that you need to do the same. In fact, I am telling you that before you make any decisions, you should talk to a licensed and qualified financial counselor as well as your divorce attorney. That way you know you are receiving competent qualified advice. However, look ahead a bit and start thinking about how you can pile up cash to make sure that money is not one of the crises that you are going to have to face. You won't be sorry for planning ahead a bit.

Taking Refuge In A Hotel

After my wife announced that she wanted a divorce and had left our house, I found it very hard to be there. There were reminders of our seemingly happy life everywhere and it hurt to look at them. I could escape and go to work, but sometimes I needed to get away and hide to keep my sanity. A hotel offered the perfect escape for me and you should not be afraid to check into one for a night or two.

Inside the four anonymous walls of a hotel room, sometimes I could even forget what was going on in my life and just get a quiet night's sleep. I won't say it was entirely healthy, but sometimes I would just pretend that I was on a business trip and everything was alright at home. I would close my eyes, go to sleep (often with the aid of some prescription sleeping pills my doctor had prescribed), and wake up a little more refreshed than I would have been had a spent a sleepless night at home.

A hotel isn't the only option. Maybe a friend of yours has a ski cabin, or your family has a lake house. Maybe your parents or friends have a spare bedroom that you can crash in for a night. Wherever you wind up, it is completely normal and understandable if you want to get away from your house for a bit and recharge your batteries.

How To Keep Your Mind From Racing

I have an overactive mind that I have often had trouble turning off. It can keep me up turning over the day's triumphs and defeats and what lays ahead. However, it spun into overdrive at all the prospects, possibilities and challenges of a divorce. Honestly, I couldn't slow it down enough to sleep and the lack of sleep would cause anxiety that just fed the problem. It was a self destructive and torturous cycle.

I first turned to prescription sleep aids to deal with this problem. They would put me to sleep for a few hours and I would wake up and start the process all over again. This is how it went for a few months.
Then I discovered a method to turn off my mind on my own. It was much healthier.

I would go and work out shortly before bed. I would already be tired from working during the day, and this would move me more into the realm of both mental and physical exhaustion. It would also move me closer to falling asleep. I would lie down and if my mind began to race (frequently) I would start repeating the Lord's Prayer over and over in my head. I was raised Catholic (not currently practicing) and this was a familiar mantra. I would just keep repeating the prayer over and over in my head and the white noise would drown out the racing mind. Eventually I would fall asleep. It took a while for me to get really good at this, but eventually the practice paid off and the racing became less and less of a problem.

Get Rid Of Any Guns

I am a gun owner and I have been ever since Hurricane Katrina in 2005. I like to keep a gun in the house for personal protection. However, this was a luxury that I could not afford after my divorce started. You should realize that right now too.

For me, the risk was two-fold. I was going to harm myself one night or I was going to harm someone else some other night. A gun is an easy way to do both and I wouldn't take the risk.

So one morning I packed up my gun and took it over to my my parent's house. I asked them to hold onto it for a while and to not give it back to me even if I asked. They were only too happy to accommodate as they had been worried about it too.

I also made sure to tell my wife that this had happened. I wanted to try and calm down the situation and this seemed to help a bit. It didn't fix anything, but it definitely didn't ma things worse. A gun in the house could have.

If you are a gun owner and you are going through a divorce, take and place your guns somewhere safe and out of reach. Late nights and bad thoughts do not go well with guns in the house and you just can't take the risk. Look at this as a necessary investment in your survival and the protection of yourself and others. It's the right thing to do. At this point it is more likely that you will harm someone with a gun than you will use it to protect yourself.

Get All Your Paperwork Together

The first night that my wife told me that she wanted a divorce, I was stunned. She calmly left the house and I was all alone. I was close to panic and a bit out of my mind. I don't remember a lot that happened. That doesn't surprise me. However, I do remember one bit.

I went into my office and I began looking over the papers for the mortgage. I don't know what I was looking for. I looked over everything. I didn't accomplish much, but I was on the right track.

One thing that quickly became apparent to me is how much paperwork there is in getting divorced. You need mortgage documents to refinance and marriage licenses to file your paperwork with the county. You will need tax documents and bank statements. You need to be able to show values of investments at the time of marriage and property tax statements. It's a bit daunting.

I went through and I found as much as I could. I dug through piles and boxes and filing cabinets and organized everything. No bureaucrat in the world would have found fault with the job I did. Since I wasn't sleeping I had a lot of time to kill.

You should follow my lead here. Get every type of official document and collate and organize them. You may need them in discussions with your attorney, your wife's attorney, a tax preparer, a county clerk or a divorce judge. You and your wife may stop talking and the only way to get the info you need is to have the documentation at your fingertips. Do this as soon as you feel able and you will be well prepared for all the paperwork that you are going to need to complete to move past this ugly chapter in your life.

One idea I may add is, once you have all of your documents, make another set. This was you can quickly and conveniently give a set to your wife if you and your attorney decide this is necessary.

Change All Your Passwords

This is another important precaution to take in the early part of your divorce. Unfortunately, like I have already said, you can no longer trust your wife. You are going to need to make sure that you can conduct business like emails and banking without any fear of her intruding. You especially need to protect your email boxes. These can contain very sensitive information, like communications with your divorce attorney. You certainly don't want her reading these.

Sit down and make a list of all your accounts. This list should include, at a minimum:

- Online bank accounts
- Credit Cards
- Emails
- Online payment systems (think PayPal)

Create an entirely new password. Make sure that it is not one that you have ever used. Also, make sure that it is a password that she will not be able to guess. Find or create something obscure and inscrutable. This will make sure your new secret password remains secret. Also, do yourself a favor and write this password down, somewhere where she will not find it. I found my memory was adversely affected by the emotional strain, the stress and the lack of sleep.

Ensure Anything You Care About Is Safe

It is hard to say, and even harder to accept, but when a couple is in the middle of a divorce crisis, they can no longer trust one another. The bond of fidelity is broken and people do some really despicable things to one another. Sometimes, a couple is just bent on upsetting one another and takes to destroying, selling or stealing important possessions from each other.

A friend of mine had their grandfather's coin collection stolen and sold by their estranged wife. He was devastated by this. I made sure that this was not going to happen to me.

One of the first things that I did to protect myself and important assets was to go out and rent a large safe deposit box at a commercial bank. The whole thing cost less than $50. I was the only person who had access to this box.

I put everything that was valuable and important to me into this box. This included some jewelry, antiques, some gold and important documents. Other stuff in the house was replaceable. Knowing that everything that was irreplaceable was locked up helped me to sleep better.

Now, this is not an invitation to take what is no yours or to hide anything from your wife. As to specifics as to what you can and cannot put in a safe deposit box, consult your attorney.

Open An Individual Bank Account

As a simple necessity you are going to need an individual bank account. One that your wife does not have access to. You should go out and open this right away. Now, as far as taking money out of jointly held accounts, you need to talk to your attorney about this. The same holds true for paychecks, dividends, rents, royalties and the like. However, you are going to need a place where you can put your money safely, and that you can pay bills out of. A jointly held account will never work for this and can wind up leaving you high and dry if your wife decides to take all of your money. Go out and get one of these right away.

Don't Hide Money

When my divorce first developed I went into a panic over money. I was suddenly overwhelmed with fear about being able to pay for my house alone, pay my bills, debts, and get set up in a new life. I pulled out mortgage papers and bank statements and I poured over them making sure I knew everything and wouldn't be surprised by anything. That was fine.

Another thing that I did was think about how I could go about hiding my savings from my wife to protect it in the event the divorce went bad. I researched and connived and plotted ways to hide everything.

In the end, hiding money wasn't necessary, but that didn't matter. I was glad that I hadn't hid anything. In the event that a divorce becomes contentious, hiding money can become a serious problem. It can also land you into deep water with a divorce judge, as well as, it is illegal in most situations.

For me, the thought of hiding money was a knee jerk reaction, but it could have been a horrible mistake. If you have assets that are worth protecting and you want to make sure they remain with you, your attorney is the one to talk to. Talk to them A.S.A.P. They can offer you correct advice as to what is legal and permissible, as well as what can cause you to wind up in deeper legal water. They are your legal counselor and you need to trust them. Don't succumb to any harebrained schemes.

Make & Stash A Keepsake Box

One of the first instincts that I had when I was confronted with the divorce was to destroy everything that was connected to my marriage or reminded me of it. It got so bad that I even burned my marriage certificate.

I regretted that even before the flames had faded, but it was gone. It was a sobering moment about myself, and it showed how far I would go to express my pain.

I was afraid that in a fit of despair, I might to the same thing again to photo albums and gifts from my wife. As angry as I was, I knew then, that I would regret it later if I did. So I made a safe box.

All of the stuff that I wanted to protect was too big for a safe deposit box. Instead, I threw it all in a big moving box and I drove it over to a friend's house. I had taped the box shut for privacy. I asked him to hold onto it until I came to get it from him. I asked him to just keep it safe. He did, like a faithful friend.

Once the dust had settled and my emotions were less raw, I went and got the box back from him. Everything in it was safe and sound, and I was glad that I had protected these things.

I would recommend doing the same thing in your divorce. Take everything that was important in your marriage, or represents your marriage and stash them in a safe house. Removing them will help you to cope a bit, and you will be glad later that you saved them. Don't throw it all away right now while your passion and emotions are running so high. If you still want to throw everything away, you always can later.

Don't Forget Your Credit

One of the most overlooked business aspects of a divorce is the couple's credit. While you are still married, you and your wife share a credit history. You may share joint accounts, and you probably have mutual credit agreements, like a mortgage. This can present a huge liability. For example, you and your wife share a credit card. She runs of to the tropics with a new lover and maxes out the card. This creates two potential problems. The first is that you are no longer in control of a financial resource. If she uses it all up and you need the credit, what are you supposed to do? Additionally, because your name is still on the account, you may wind up having to pay for her love jaunt, no matter what the divorce judge says just to save your credit. No one should have to do that.

Well, there are some things you can do to tidy up and batten down the hatches for the coming storm. The first order of business to to get a copy of your credit report. I would recommend signing up for a credit monitoring service through your divorce. These will give you alerts if anything weird happens, as well as give you access to your three bureau credit score on a monthly basis. That last bit is important. Whatever service you sign up with, make sure you get access to all three reports from the three credit bureaus (Experian, Equifax and Transunion for the record).

Once you get your report sit down and study it. Determine what the status of every account is. Also, look for anything you don't recognize. It is sad to say, but you can't trust your wife at this point, so look for anything out of place. If you find anything, make sure you know exactly what it is before moving on.

If you have any joint accounts, consider closing them after you consult with your attorney to make sure this is OK. In some cases, you may not be able to because of an outstanding balance. If that is the case, contact the finance company and discuss your situation with them. See what they can do. In some cases they may be able to remove your name from accounts or close accounts and issue new ones. Essentially, you are trying to limit the impact your now estranged wife can have on your finances. You are not trying to hurt her or disrupt her life in anyway, you just want to make sure you are in control of your resources. You of course will be doing this in concert with your qualified attorney.

The last step you may want to consider is to put a security freeze on your credit files. This is a lock on your accounts to make sure that no fraudulent accounts can be opened. Again, unfortunately you cannot trust your spouse at this point. As such, she does have access to very sensitive materials and identity theft is not out of the question. To issue a security freeze, you will need to contact each of the three credit bureaus in writing, via registered mail. For more information, visit www.experian.com, www.equifax.com, and www.transuion.com.

Once you have completed this step, your finances are a little more secure. You have achieved a step that will offer your life some stability, at least financially speaking.

Talking To Your Boss

Talking to your boss is an important discussion that you need to have with yourself when your divorce first starts. Be honest with yourself. Your home life is a mess and your heart may be in tatters. A lot of people (including me) throw themselves into their work. However, since their soul is not really involved in their work and their mind is always drifting to the mess that they still have not cleaned up, their work product may suffer. You should admit this and accept it, it's true.

I did talk to my boss and I was fortunate enough to have a caring supervisor. The first thing he did was offer me some personal time. I really appreciated the offer, and honestly, the last thing I wanted was time off. I was already dreading the vacation time that loomed a few weeks down the road. When I was home, all I thought of was my misery. Work at least distracted me.

I told him that I would tough it out, but I asked a favor of him. I asked him to pay special attention to my work performance (I was in a sales management job at the time) and let me know if he noted and deterioration. He said that he would. He also did his job and made sure that I knew about our company health plan EAP. He didn't know that I had been talking to them almost every night for a week at that point.

I will not offer you advice as to whether or not to talk to your supervisor. I am not qualified to do that. What I will do, however, is tell you that you need to decide whether or not you are going to talk to your boss ahead of time. Make the decision before you are forced to do so and have a plan. Only you know our situation and what is best for you.

Prescription Medications

I have never been a big fan of prescription medication. When I am given pain pills, I rarely take them. However, this did not stop me from trying to cope with with the pain and anxiety I felt with prescription medication. Of course, these were prescribed to me by my doctor.

I went to my doctor and told her what had happened. She talked to me about options and how I was doing. We identified to main problems. First, I couldn't get through the day without waves of panic. These of course are normal in this situation. I also told her I couldn't sleep. Even over the counter medications couldn't put me to sleep and I was wary of taking more than the package said.

After we talked she told me that she would prescribe me two things. The first was a sleep aid and the other was an anti anxiety.

I went through a couple different sleep aids before I found one that wasn't habit forming and allowed me to sleep. If you are taking a sleep aid, pay close attention to any side effects. The first one I took, honestly gave me hallucinations, I am pretty certain I sleep walked and I sent text messages to my ex-wife that I had no memory of. None of these effects were helpful. I communicated these effects to my doctor and ultimately, we found one that did work without the troubles. Honestly, I don't think I could have gotten enough sleep to stay sane through this crisis without the pills. I don't take them now, but they were a lifesaver to me then.

The anti-anxiety pills are another story. I stopped taking them very quickly. The effects of these pills were extremely noticeable. The made me spacey and lethargic. I didn't like the effect of these pills at all. I was afraid to drive and working was much harder. I had not focus to my mind (I'm assuming that was the point). I decided that this was not how I wanted to live and I did stop taking these.

When I told all this to my doctor, she agreed that I should stop taking the anti-anxiety. She said that talk therapy, like I was doing with my counselor had been shown to reduce anxiety as well. I decided that my weekly counseling sessions would be enough to deal with the anxiety.

Whatever medications you and your doctor decide are for you, I would recommend paying attention and making notes on their effect. Some of them may be helpful to you, and others may not be. Don't be afraid to make the decision that some medications aren't right for you. However, as always, discuss this with your doctor beforehand and never self medicate.

Conclusion
The steps and ideas that were listed in this chapter are not intended to make your world all better. That is only going to happen with time. These steps, however, in conjunction with the coping techniques that are listed in the next chapter, will help you to cope with the strain you are now under, as well as begin the healing process. You are well on your way to making it through the unhappy process that is divorce. Take credit for getting this far. You're doing great.

Chapter 3
Developing Coping Techniques

Once you have stabilized your situation and you have all of your support system built and you have put all your affairs in order, you are still not done. Like I have said before in this book, divorce takes time. I certainly felt like I existed in some kind of limbo, stuck between two worlds. I wasn't really a married man, and at the same time I wasn't quite a single man. I didn't want to start dating until everything was finished up between my wife and I. I wanted to keep that door open. I also still had a very wounded heart and soul and I needed to breathe a bit of happiness back into my life.

What I needed were techniques to help me pass time and have fun, as well as ease my mental burden, in a way that did not create new stresses in my life. That is the subject of this chapter. In the pages that follow, I will discuss all of the tips and tricks that I used to help pass time, have fun and keep me distracted. I also used these techniques to help me deal with stress, loneliness, depression, heartbreak, and all the other negative repercussions of my divorce crisis. As usual, it is my hope that you can learn from my experiences and develop similar methods to cope with the ongoing stress of your own divorce.

Keeping Yourself Busy

One of the biggest challenges that I experienced during my crisis was how to keep my hands and my mind busy. Idleness was my enemy. My mind would drift through my problems and my emotions would run the gamut from suicidal to enraged. It was a roller coaster experience. Keeping busy helped to level me out and keep my mind off of my problems.

I want to be clear, this wasn't running from my problems. One thing you will quickly discover in your own divorce, is that there is a lot of time where you will not have anything productive to do where your divorce is concerned. Counseling will be over, you will have talked to your lawyer, your friends and family are at work, and you are left on your own to fill the hours.

I filled it a lot of ways. I borrowed a page from Malcolm X's book at times and I sat and copied out the dictionary by hand. This was actually really helpful when I couldn't sleep and calmed me down. It also helped keep my mind from racing.

I also volunteered during the early parts of my divorce. This was especially helpful as the positive influence I was having helped buoy my spirits. It also allowed me to get out and socialize with people that didn't know about my divorce. When I was with people that did know about the divorce, the conversation always went to that subject. However, with these anonymous folks, conversation wasn't deep. It was just friendly idle chat.

I also set myself to performing lots of chores around the house. I cleaned everything that had ever needed cleaning or had been forgotten about. I repaired the deck. I put in a new lawn. I planted flowers and pruned trees. I laugh now, but I even went out and bought a floor polisher for the hardwood floors. At times, if you had come to my house early in my divorce, you would have found me at four in the morning, stripped to the waist on my knees scrubbing linoleum with a hand brush. Anything to keep my mind busy.

Your job can fill a lot of the time in your week, but remember, it can't fill it all. You are going to need to come up with a list of activities that you can do on your own to keep yourself busy. Do what you like and gives you peace. Go fishing, carve wood, work on your car, clean, volunteer, or copy pages out of the dictionary. Just make sure you come up with something. It is a basic coping skill you can rely on.

Force Yourself To Be Social

Along with finding ways to fill your off hours with positive activities, you need to force yourself to be social.

I really had to force myself to see my friends and family. Now, this is not to say that they are bad company, quite the opposite. However, while I was working through my divorce crisis, there were long periods where I didn't want to be around anyone. I was exhausted and miserable, and all I really wanted to do was wallow in my own misery until I could fall asleep or pass out.

I realized this within the first month of the crisis. I made a resolution to force myself to be social. I would accept any invitation I was given no matter how much

I wanted to go home and crawl into bed. Fortunately I got a lot of invitations and my friends kept me pretty busy. They were great.

This wound up being a huge help to me. I got out and usually had a great time. I would talk to other people. Some of them were divorced and we would compare notes. Some of them were single and seeing them would remind me that I could be single too. I even tried my hand at innocent flirting a time or two.

The overall benefit to being social is manifold to me. First it helped me to avoid the pitfall of depression. Being around other people made me feel better. When I was alone misery and despair seemed to creep into my head much easier. When I was with others these emotions would tend to keep their distance. Also being in a group and getting out to do things helped to remind me that life wasn't over with my divorce. I remembered that life would go on and I would have fun at the same time.

When I went home and finally did go to bed after having spent times with friends and family, I was usually even more tired than when I had left, but I always felt better and could fall asleep much easier as a result.

Get out there and do the same. Force yourself to be social.

Writing Stuff Down

For about one year after my divorce crisis started, my mind was a jumble. I have always prided myself on cool rational and logical thought. However, this went out the window quickly and didn't return for some time. A thought would enter my head about counseling, and before I could wrap my head around it, something else had taken its place, and it was gone.

I found that what I needed to do was to carry a small notebook with me. This allowed me to write down thoughts I was having when I had them, so I could look back over them at a more convenient time. Usually these thoughts about counseling, chores I had to do to make sure my household and affairs stayed in line, or discussions that I wanted to have with my estranged wife.

I found this practice to be amazingly helpful in terms of organizing my ideas. It improved my ability to cope, my therapy sessions and communication with my wife. I would recommend that you follow my lead and start taking notes on your life.

Mood Journals

I found one of the exercises that my second counselor gave me to be so helpful that I want to relay the concept here to you. I am doing this as it may have not come up yet in your counseling sessions, or you may have disregarded my previous advice and you may not be in counseling. This is also an extension of my advice to write stuff down.

This homework assignment was the "mood journal". It's a simple idea. Throughout the day, usually on the hour, I would write a few quick notes on how I was feeling. Specifically my mood. How did I feel? Did I feel optimistic? Did I feel hopeless?

This helped me to understand how I was feeling throughout the day and it allowed me to recognize patterns of when I would feel lonely, isolated, and hopeless. In short, it allowed me to see when I experienced periods of negative feelings throughout the day.

This proved to be very helpful to me in terms of helping to manage these negative feelings. Now, negative feelings in a divorce are very much to be expected. However, I found that I would become susceptible to these feelings much more at certain periods of the day. For example, in the late afternoons, I would often experience heightened negative emotions. This was largely due to the fact that I was tired from the work day and was experiencing low blood sugar. By using the mood journal, I was able to identify pitfalls like this one and I could more effectively cope with these feeling and help to prevent them. For example, in the late afternoons, I would make sure to have a snack. In addition to moods, I was also asked to track my sleep patterns and to write down any dreams I was having. Again, this helped me recognize patterns and to develop strategies to cope with them. The dream journal also helped me to explore more subtle emotions, like fear of abandonment, in counseling.

All of this self-observation and recording of information allowed my counselor and I to see a much more comprehensive view of my state of well being. This in turn, helped us to deal with specific issues that greatly increased my ability to cope and rebuild my life. I would strongly recommend similar self-observation to you!

Turn Yourself Over To A Higher Power

In twelve step programs all around the world, people recite the serenity prayer. This prayer is simply a prayer God (not specific which one) for support in dealing with their crises – whatever they may be.

In my divorce crisis, throughout the whole thing, I recited my own version of a serenity prayer. It became a very important part of my coping skills. This is not a book about religion, and I certainly am not here to preach or proselytize, but I would recommend, as a means of coping, that you say your own prayer whenever you are stressed, lonely, despondent, feeling abandoned or are otherwise feeling the weight of the burden you are carrying.

My own prayer was simple. I asked God for five things to help me survive my ordeal. Every time they were the same. The five things were:

    ⊼   Strength – To carry on and rebuild my life

- Courage – To face the challenges that lay ahead
- Wisdom – To understand how I was feeling and to see the truth in things
- Patience – A divorce is a long process that often takes much longer than you would think reasonable. Patience is absolutely necessary.
- Grace – To forgive and work towards healing myself, my family and the people who care about me.

This was my prayer and I am including it merely as an example. Look inside your heart and decide what you need and what will help you to forgive, move on and rebuild your life. Pray for it when you are in bad places or times of struggle.

Exercise Is Great

My first counselor recommended to me that I get some exercise as one of my coping skills. I won't lie, I had never really been an exercise person up to that point.

I was willing to try anything so I went out and joined a gym. That didn't work. I was wrestling with depression at the time and the last thing I really wanted to do was leave the house to go feel husky in a room full of beautiful people. I kept the gym membership, I just never went.

What I did instead was go to my local thrift store and buy a ski machine and a rowing machine. They cost me all of $20. They weren't the latest and greatest but I could set them up in the privacy of my own home and I could work out on them until I was exhausted.

I would work out on these machines until I dripped sweat and I felt like my heart was going to explode. But, I noticed a few positive changes that I attributed to the machines.

First, when I worked out I noticed that my mood seemed to be better. I would feel more positive about the mess my life had become. Seriously. I would feel more able to address my problems and this was a huge help. Secondly, I found that I slept better. I would work out on those machines for a couple of hours and be physically exhausted, with a more positive mood. This would help me sleep and the added sleep only further helped my mood. Lastly, when I was on the machines, I found that my mind drifted away from the problems of my life and I just spaced out. This was huge to me too. An hour where I didn't think about my divorce was rare and I got on the machines in the hope of more.

I strongly recommend that you work some kind of physical exercise plan into your divorce survival plan too. It can be simple and you don't have to spend a lot of money. Buy a jump rope if money or space are limited. I bought a jump rope when I was in my apartment (more on that later) and it would achieve all of the same effects. Get out with friends and play basketball. Go for a run. Just do something physical to take your mind of things and put your mental compass on a good setting.

Get Outdoors

One of the best ways I found to take my mind off of my problems and recharge my batteries was to get outside. Literally, just being out of doors made me feel better in general. My mood was elevated and I felt much more positive about the challenges that lay ahead of me and my life.

In the area where I live there are lots of options for outdoor recreation. Mountains, parks, lakes and rivers are all very close by and are easily accessible. I took walks and hikes. I kayaked. I went biking. All of these worked for me and offered a real addition to just working out.

If space is limited, or you are in an urban environment, you have two options. You can get out of town and go rough it for a bit. This is only possible if your life permits it and you have the time to spend. However, you can always just go for walks in your neighborhood.

As an exercise, get out of your home and go walk 20 city blocks. In most cases this is about two miles. The whole process shouldn't take more than half an hour or so. As yourself when you are done, how you are felling? Do you feel better than you did? My experience suggest to me that you will.

Misery Loves Company – Divorce Buddies

In my personal situation, as I talked with my friends and acquaintances about my divorce, I was amazed how many of them were eager to talk about their own divorces. These people seemed to rise like stalks of corn in a late Summer sun. I was amazed. I had never known about the past or present divorces that many of my friends were going through. It seemed that now that I had my own, I was a member of the club. These people liked to talk about their divorces and I would listen and I would talk about mine and they would listen.

We would keep each other informed as to the progress of the divorce. We would talk about snags that we had hit along the way. We would compare notes, and as the bonds grew deeper, we would talk about our feelings. These conversations, at times, became very personal indeed and often involved a great deal of trust and personal knowledge. I truly valued, then and now, the openness, honesty and connection that I experienced in these relationships.

These conversations and newly intimate friendships were valuable to me for many reasons. They showed that the path I was walking was one trod on by many people. People I had known for a long time were also secretly walking through the same hardships I was. Hell, it was nice to feel that I wasn't alone. I am sure that is one of the reasons many of these people opened up to me. It was also nice to compare divorces. In some cases, I learned tips and tricks that helped to simplify my own proceedings. In many cases, these conversations and lunches became little one on one support groups.

This type of opportunity may have been unique to me. I'm honestly not sure to this day. For some reason, in my life, people have always opened up to me. I feel honored when they do. These relationships may have just developed from that. However, you too may encounter this phenomenon in your divorce. Watch for it and watch for the opportunities to present themselves. If they do, approach them with an open mind and see what they may have to offer.

Just the other day, as I am writing this manuscript, I found that it was my turn to fulfill this role for another person. They told me about their own marital difficulties and I talked freely about my own divorce. In the end, they thanked me and said it was good just to talk to someone who has been there. I smiled and laughed a bit while I thought of how everything really does come full circle.

Peer Support Groups

The intimate connection with another person, by chance, that I described above may come your way. It may not. I depends both on fate and you. However, you can go out and look for the opportunity to talk with others who are living in the same difficulties that you are and those who have walked through the fire. You can do this through a peer support group. If you can't find one in your area, you can even start your own.

If you live in a large city, there is almost certainly one, if not many divorce support groups. Churches are frequent sponsors of these events. They may even be divided into men's and women's groups.

A great resource for this kind of thing is a website called meetup.com. This is a social organization website that is very helpful for getting people with similar interests together. I would strongly recommend that you, at the very least, search this website for groups in your area. More than likely you will find one.

I went to a group in my area. I actually went a few times. I found it beneficial, but it was at a time that was inconvenient for me, with work. Plus, I had already built a strong support group through all my divorce buddies, my family, my counselor and my brain trust. So, I will confess, I did stop going. All that aside, I did at least explore the options at my disposal. I would strongly recommend that you do the same.

Redecorating To Ease Stress

One of the hardest challenges I faced during my divorce was making peace with my home. Everything about it reminded me of my marriage and the divorce that was quickly becoming an all consuming problem. For a while, I simply found the problem of my house and living in it overwhelming and did move into an apartment for a spell. I also held out hope for a reconciliation with my wife and was not in a huge hurry to disrupt things in the event this happened.

Eventually I needed to face the facts that I needed to live in my house, but I needed to make it a place that I could be comfortable in. A friend of mine suggested that I redecorate a bit to make it seem like a new space and I took her advice to heart.

I did a lot of redecorating before I was done. I painted walls, and moved my bedroom to a space that I had never associated with the intimacy of marriage. This created a bedroom where I could sleep a little easier.

I also rearranged furniture and hung new art. When I was done, the house looked completely different then it had during my marriage.

This step allowed me to have the feeling of a fresh start and I credit it largely for my being able to live in this house to this day.

Build A Safe Zone

One early realization in my divorce crisis was the sad fact that my home had ceased to be my home. It had turned into a shrine to past memories. Everywhere I looked I found pictures and reminders of a life past. It was intolerable at times. It also had become a battle-ground. My wife and I still owned the home and were in the process of squabbling over items in it. We fought constantly. In the beginning, at times, I felt that I was going to snap. I mean that in every way you can conceive. Good and very bad. Something had to give. It turns out that it was me. I left.

I had spent a few nights in hotels to get away in the beginning. However, I made the monumental decision to turn my back on what had been a happy home to establish a new one. I sought to create not only a home, but a safe haven where I could ride out the storm that I sensed my divorce was going to be.

I went out and found the perfect spot. It was an apartment designed for students near a college. It came furnished with all utilities included in the rent. It was a month to month lease. It was the perfect turn key option for college freshman and marriage refugees like myself.

The best part of all was that my name didn't appear anywhere except on the lease. There was no phone in my name. The utilities weren't in my name. Nothing. It would have been damn hard for anyone to find me there. I kept it a secret. It was my secret base. I laugh now, but it made me feel like a secret agent to have my own little safe house. But, it was perfect.

I wound up spending about six months in this safe house. There were no memories to trouble me and I noticed that my sleep immediately started improving. The most important asset that I bought by fleeing my own home was perspective, however. Getting away from the constant din and thunder of the divorce allowed me to step back and look at the big picture. The quiet allowed my mind time to think and process and it allowed my feelings to normalize. I would make the same decision now if I had it all to do over. I would also recommend that, if you are able to, that you should establish your own safe house.

Now, before you go and turn yourself into a secret agent, you do need to discuss the ramifications of this decision with your attorney. In many cases, a decision like this could have repercussions regarding your rights to property in your divorce settlement. This is a very real aspect that needs to be considered and you need to know all the options you have. However, if your attorney green lights the idea, set up your own little base and step back for a bit. I am quite certain, if nothing else, you will get more sleep. This alone is worth it.

Email Is A Great Way To Communicate

I am going to tell you right now that I hate text messages. I find them to be a means of communication that does a very bad job of communicating. I use them as little as I can. When I was going through my divorce this seemed to be the only way that my wife would talk to me at time. It made me angry and confused me a lot. I could never really get what she was saying. The subtlety and the non-verbal communication was stripped away to leave me in doubt of what was really meant. Finally one day I just had enough.

I told her that I was not going to communicate through text messages anymore. However, we couldn't be in the same place at this point and we needed a way to talk. Phone conversations just fell apart into arguments that were not productive or fun. So I proposed email and this worked fairly well.

Email has a lot of positives as far as a communication medium in a divorce. First, it can be long enough to fully explain your meaning. Text messages confine you to 150 characters and this is simply not enough to explain a complex idea. Secondly, email is delayed. You don't have to respond to anything right away like you do with a phone conversation. This helps cut down on getting angry. Additionally, email is imper- sonal. Since you do not have contact with the person like face to face or over the phone, you can say things that may be hard. This makes conversations easier to have as the emotional component is removed.

Another great function of email communication is that it allows you to consider what you wrote later before sending it. I would often write emails to my wife and save them as drafts. Then I would give myself 24 hours and see if I still wanted to send it. If I did off it went, and if I did not, I delete it. I deleted more emails than I sent actually.

The last benefit of email may come in handy later on in your divorce process. This is that emails create a re- cord of communication. There are laws that govern re- cording phone conversation and text messages can eas- ily be erased. However, emails will sit in your inbox until you erase them. This is a simple precaution, but your lawyer may find a need or use for any communic- ation records if the divorce becomes adversarial. You never know, so start planning ahead now.

Talking To Yourself Doesn't Mean Your Crazy

When I was growing up, anyone who was talking to themselves was automatically crazy. Let me tell you, I talk to myself all the time and I am not crazy. This was especially true during my divorce.

I would be alone in my apartment and my mind would be spinning. Well, it often helped me to work through the ideas and thoughts that I was having by voicing them out loud. I could bounce ideas around much more easily than I could if they were in my head. Also, sometimes saying things out loud helped me to embrace them a little better. For example, "I am going to get a divorce". When this phrase is in your head, it is easy to pretend that it is not real, saying it out loud makes it much more real and forced me to deal with it.

Also, in times of stress people will often work out ideas verbally on their own. Let me just assure you that this does not mean that you are crazy. Far from it actually. This means that you are processing both emotions and thoughts in a healthy manner.

Just make sure you do it when you are alone. Driving to and from work is a perfect time!

Have Some Fun...It's OK

Divorce has the very nasty habit of taking a some-times very happy people and turning their lives upside down. Where once your life had been about BBQs and vacations, now you find that it is about attorney appointments and counseling sessions and crying fits. It is no fun at all.

Well, it is going to be up to you to inject a little colorful joy into the gray landscape of your life. Only you can do it. I tried to do it a lot. Every chance I got actually.

I pampered myself at times. I developed a taste for pedicures. Don't laugh until you've tried it. They're actually amazingly relaxing. I sky dived. I recreated in my off time. I boated, rode motorcycles and fished.

I also went on a vacation during that horrible year. That's right. In the middle of my divorce, I left the country and spent some time on a tropical beach. Being 3000 miles from my problems did have it's tonic effect.

In the case of my vacation, I used that as a reward. I had finally refinanced the house and I had filed the final divorce papers. All that was left was to wait out the waiting period that is required by my state. It had been a rough month and I had had to work hard to get everything done and still keep my job too. I was tired in body and soul and it still wasn't over. I still had to face the final hearing and any surprises that might have popped up along the way. So, I used the vacation as a reward for the hard work and a chance to recharge my batteries for the final push that lay ahead.

Consider rewarding yourself with something fun when you have reached a milestone. Psychologically, it will help to keep you going in that push to the end. Also, it will give you something to look forward to and will help to keep you motivated. You need to have some fun in your life, but you can also use it as a motivator to get this whole process over with.

Create A New Routine

It's been remarked that living in prison is made simpler by having a routine. The mind tends to find comfort in simple habits that offer it comfort and predictability. If you are facing a divorce, your life has suddenly become anything but predictable. The common, comfortable habits that you and your wife shared are suddenly gone.

For me, one of the hardest changes was not having my wife greet me when I came home from work. Every night when I would come home, she would greet me with a hug and a kiss. It was simple and mundane, and I took how much it meant to me for granted. When it was gone I felt its absences like a cold winter wind on my face.

There were many other changes that I suddenly had to cope with that were new and unwelcome. I would often find new ones and I found that this unpredictability was hellish. I couldn't make the pain or loneliness go away, but I could create a new routine to help my mind cope with these changes and find comfort. I did just that.

I started making sure that I exercised everyday. I even did so in the same fashion every day. Treadmill, then stair stepper, then rowing machine. I would work out for the same amount of time every day. I did the laundry on Saturdays and I cleaned the house on Sundays and then played golf with a friend who was very patient and helpful. Each weekend, no excuses. I had also taken to eating a lot of take away food in the living room rather than cooking dinner and eating it at the kitchen table like I we had done when our marriage was good. It was a little hard. I forced myself to start cooking and eating dinner in the kitchen, although I did offer myself the concession of adding a TV and DVD player so I could watch movies when I dined alone. This made the kitchen more comfortable, and again, did not take away the negative feelings I had, but at least allowed me a way to cope with them. Remember, if you listen to music while the dentist is drilling, you still know they're drilling, you can just cope with it a little better.

Work very hard to establish routine in your life. It will help you cope. Don't stop doing the things you do on a regular basis. If you go to the gym on Mondays, Wednesdays and Fridays, don't stop. If you cook dinner or breakfast keep doing it. If you spend time with friends and family regularly make a point to keep those dates. Force yourself to maintain a routine even if you don't feel like it. The continuity of the routines in your life, as well as the addition of new one will go a long way to providing you with stability, comfort and a way to cope with all the feelings you have and the difficulties you will face.

Sleep Is Essential

Dealing with the strain of a divorce is going to wear you down. This is especially true if everything else in your life is going to continue (in most cases it has to). You will be working, and taking care of your personal and family responsibilities just like before, but now, you will have lots of business and emotional stress that needs to be attended to. All of this is going to drain your physical, emotional and mental reserves.

Sleep is the natural way that your body replenishes these reserves and you are going to need plenty of it. When I was first dealing with all of this, I was afraid to sleep (when I could) for long periods. I was afraid that it was symptomatic of depression. If I was sleeping twelve hours a day, I thought this meant that I was running from reality, plunging into a pit of loneliness, despair, and depression.

Well, after talking with one of my counselors about the physiological and psychological need for sleep, and the way that fatigue is your body's way of warning you of low energy, I was reassured that sleeping was OK. In fact, it was more than OK. It was necessary for my health at this point, more so than ever before.

As always, I encourage you to work with a professional counselor through this crisis. However, I want to assure you that sleeping, even for longer periods than you are used to, is a completely natural way for your body to deal with the additional strain it is facing.

This is not license for you to lie awake in bed all day, everyday, but you need to know that sleeping for long periods is just fine. If you are concerned about how much you are sleeping, you can always discuss it with your counselor or medical doctor.

Mediation Is Great

In the middle of a divorce crisis your mind will often be racing all over the place. I found myself caught in all kinds of conflicting emotional battles. At one point trying to reconcile with my wife at the other plotting how I could most upset her. It was confusing to say the least and taxing emotionally. Due to all of these conflicting emotions, I found it hard at times to think clearly.

I found meditation helped me to keep my mind busy and to focus my thoughts quite a bit. I used four types of meditation and all of them were useful, just in different ways.

Firstly, I would go to a public garden in my area when I knew it would be quiet. There are many stone benches in these gardens and I would find an out of the way one and sit. I would close my eyes and just try to listen to the sounds around me. I found that this helped me quite a bit and I could even do it on my lunch break. I loved listening to the rain and that calmed and soothed me the most.

Next, I would take long walks, usually at night when I could not sleep. I found that the alone time coupled with activity allowed me to think more clearly and it helped to distract me. Now, I would not recommend doing this in every neighborhood and you need to be smart about how you do it.

When I found that my mind was overactive and was racing a mile a minute (an all too common side effect of living in a crisis like divorce), the only way that I could slow it down was to provide it with a structured, pointless activity. I have heard of people famously copying out books in prison. Malcolm X copied the dictionary when he was serving time. This seemed to me a perfect task to slow a racing mind. I chose to copy the book of Psalms from the Bible. I sat down and wrote out Psalms when I needed to slow my mind. I would do it for as long as two hours at a time and when I was done, I always felt more at peace and my mind had slowed. When I was done, I felt much more in control of myself and my emotions.

The last meditation activity that I would undertake was going to a movie. This may seem odd, but it worked great for me. I have always been a bit of a hyperactive person and I rarely am doing only one thing at a time. However, I found that by paying for a movie ticket and sitting there alone in the dark, I could just sit and check out of my life for an hour or two. I wasn't hiding for my problems, but it did allow me to push the pause button on more than one occasion. Where I live, there is an inexpensive second run movie theater. Tickets are cheap and I could always find something to watch. Taking in a flick helped me many times.

You should try to find a positive way to relax and calm yourself down. This will be crucial to coping with your divorce. Unfortunately a lot of men tend to hid from their problems, deny they exist or drink until they forget. I did all of these at least once and sometimes more than that while I coped with the shock of my divorce. However, I realized that these were not helpful and I refocused my efforts.

Just a few ideas of positive meditation like activities are:

- Take a yoga class
- Work out
- Write out a book long hand
- Go to a movie
- Sit in a garden
- Take up painting, drawing, pottery
- Plant a garden
- Go fishing
- Listen to music
- Pray

Any of these will help to clear your mind. The important thing is that you develop a technique to calm yourself when you feel anxiety begin to overwhelm you.

Safe Female Companionship

About three months into my divorce, a woman at work asked me to give her a ride home. It was just a favor and she had no other intentions. However, it had been a long, hard day, and we were both tired and hungry. I think I was too tired to let my reservations get the best of me. I asked her if she wanted to join me for dinner. You may not believe it, but I also had no intentions other than dinner.

We wound up at one of my favorite restaurants (I like them because I know they're open late) having a very nice dinner. We talked. Maybe we were both tired and we both relaxed a bit. She had just gone through a breakup and maybe she was a bit lonely too. I certainly was. Misery loves company. We wound up talking for hours. We just got to know each other. It was the kind of talk you would have on a first date, but neither of us thought of this as a date. I certainly wasn't ready. But, it felt great to just go and have dinner with a woman. Up to this point, my social time with the fairer sex had been close to zero. It felt a little odd, but it felt great at the same time. I drove her home and we parted.

On the drive home, though, I really got to thinking. I asked myself why this had been so enjoyable to me. What I realized was that I liked spending time with women and I enjoy their company. I wasn't a monk. I liked making a woman smile and talking with her. The flow and conversation was different than when I talked with my male friends. I had been sorely missing that in my life and this dinner had made me realize it.

Odder still to me, was the fact that I felt no desire to take the relationship to a more physical level. I was probably still numb from the divorce and there was still some hope in my mind for a reconciliation. Still, it was a big, first step, after nine years of marriage to be out with another woman, one on one. We saw much more of each other and this woman has become one of my very good friends even to this day.

I told you that story to illustrate a point in this book. Men have a natural desire to be around women. We like them. However, as a married man, you may have limited this to your wife during your divorce. Now that your wife is gone, you, like me, may be feeling a hole in your life and you may have a desire to start seeing women socially. There is nothing wrong with this at all, and in fact, it may be very helpful for you to start rebuilding your social life and to fine tune your dating skills in a safe way.

However, this comes with a bit of a warning. Be careful about becoming emotionally involved with another woman, while your divorce and marriage are still uncertain. One of my greatest fears during my divorce was that I would become emotionally involved with a woman, only to find my wife and I trying to reconcile. At that point, I would ultimately have to hurt someone that I cared about. Thankfully this didn't happen. This is largely due to my caution and to my keeping my relationships with women, during the uncertainty phase of my divorce, on a friend level only.

I would advise you do the same. You can always turn a friend into a lover once your situation has become more solid and your life is less uncertain. I am glad that I waited and I believe that you will be too. Waiting for something good is almost always worth it.

Get A Massage

This might seem like a bit of silly advice as your world is falling apart, but I would seriously suggest that you take an hour a week (if you can) and go and get yourself a massage. I did this regularly through my divorce and still do to this day.

This little bit of pampering and stress relief really helped me cope. I would get on the table and for one hour, check out of my world. I would just lie there and let the hands of the therapist ease all the tension away.

If cost is the issue, rather than time, there are two options I would recommend. First, if there is a massage school in your area, they will have a student clinic. These are a lot cheaper than fully licensed massages. However the massages are just as good. In my area, these set me back $25. This was more than worth the amount of relaxation that it bought me.

The second option that I might recommend is for you to talk to your doctor. It is possible to get a physicians recommendation that you receive massage as part of your medical treatment (depression and anxiety are medical issues). This will allow you to bill your insurance for massages. This can help cut the price quite a bit.

If you are just nervous about getting a massage, bite the bullet and go try one. You will not regret it. Everyone I have ever turned onto a massage has come back and thanked me.

Dealing With Loss Of Companionship

One of the hardest hurdles that I had to jump during this divorce crisis was the loss of companionship. I would have a bad day at work, and suddenly, I had no intimate partner to listen to me. I would have a great day on the golf course, and I had no one to tell the story to when I got home. It was odd. Honestly, it was like waking up one morning and finding tat you only had one arm. It felt like a piece of me was gone.

This was very hard at first, but I did cope with it. I found a way to survive that I think made me grow as a person. I started opening myself up more to existing friends and I started new deeper friendships that involved communication and support that had usually only came from my wife. Some of these friendships were with other people in the middle of their divorces, and maybe they were a tad codependent, but they were and are very helpful to me. I still cherish many of these friendships now, even after my divorce.

This tip for surviving your divorce is a hard one. If you are an introverted person, opening yourself up to new people can be hard. I know, I tend to be introverted. However, I forced myself to do it and I found wonderful personal connections once I had.

There is no road map or step by step that I can give you. The one suggestion that I would make is to be a good listener. People usually just wait for their own turn to talk and by just listening, sincerely, you help to lay the foundation for real communication. Often, once someone realizes that you are actually listening to them, they will reciprocate. More than likely, this is how the connection between you and your wife started.

Get A Furry Friend

One way to deal with the loss of companionship that a divorce is so often fraught with is to get yourself a furry friend. Animals have a way of loving you unconditionally and this is really something that is very beneficial when you find yourself alone in a divorce.

You do need to make sure that you are up to caring for an animal before you purchase one however. Do your homework and try to pick one up at the local shelter. They are less expensive and many of them have had a few hard knocks in life just like you. They are often very happy to have someone too.

I purchased a kitten in the middle of my divorce as a way to cope with the stress and the loss of my wife's companionship. She really helped on many occasions. She would just crawl into my lap, and purr. She didn't ask anything from me other than to spend some time with her. It was much easier and calming than being with other people. This is not to say that I was antisocial. I still spent lots of time with both friends and family, but the kitten was always there when I got to my empty house and made it feel a lot more comfortable and homey.

Dealing With No Sex

One of the hardest challenges in my divorce was dealing with no sex. I won't lie and say that I don't have a
natural, healthy sexual appetite. I do. When I was
married we would engage in sex frequently. Sex is
more than just an orgasm, it is a connection with another person and an expression of connection. Orgasm
also releases endorphins and dopamine that help to
regulate your mood. There are a lot of benefits to regular sex and the sudden end of it is something that is
definitely worth addressing in this book.

I also will not say that the loss of sex didn't seriously
affect me. At first, my guts were too torn up for sex to
really be a possibility. My mind was anything but focused, and sex took a back seat. This isn't always the
case though. For some men I have talked to, sex gets
moved to the forefront. They use it as a way to escape.
I definitely can understand this approach too. I just
didn't experience it. You may experience either of
these, or any combination of them. Either way, you
need some coping skills.

In this introduction to this book, I promised you openness and honesty. Well, here it is. When my sex drive
did return, I turned to frequent masturbation. This
helped a bit. It would be what I imagine methadone is
to a heroin addiction. It wasn't the same thing, and I
knew it. However, it helped me cope and get through
my day. There is nothing wrong with you taking this
same approach. In fact, I would recommend it. It will

help with your mood and it will help you to cope as well.

One man that I talked to about his divorce was thinking out loud about hiring a prostitute. I thought about the same thing and ultimately decided not to for a few reasons. One, it is generally illegal, and legal trouble, especially if you have kids is not what you need. Two, it can be dangerous, not to mention exploitative. Many prostitutes are simply runaways and minors who are being forced into that lifestyle by others. You should not support that. Lastly, it will not fill the void you are feeling and your need for real companionship. In the end, I have heard empirically, it will just leave you feeling even more empty and alone.

Unfortunately, I cannot offer you a quick fix to this problem. What I wanted most was connection and intimacy all wrapped up in sex and there was no way to get that without an underlying relationship. What I did was accept this. I also pledged to myself that I would not engage in sex for six months. I took a pause and allowed my emotions to heal a bit before I even thought about sex with another person. I would recommend to anyone to follow that path. It was hard as hell, but in the long run, I sincerely believe that it allowed me time to get perspective and to be ready when the right time and person did come along.

Conclusion

In this chapter, I have laid out all of the coping techniques that I learned during my divorce. This toolbox was what allowed me to survive, set aside my stress and focus on the business of healing. This does not mean that you cannot develop your own techniques, however, these will give you an excellent place to start . That is what I needed, most. I hope that these help you.

Epilogue – After Your Divorce

A friend of mine was in a horrible car accident a few years ago. He was terribly injured and spent months recovering and learning to walk again. He still walks with a limp to this day. He has told me he thinks of the accident everyday of his life. Well, I wish I could tell you differently, but a divorce is the emotional version of that accident.

You will have scars when all is said and done and every now and again, the trauma can come back hard. It was like that the first Christmas after my divorce. One minute I was fine, the next I found myself crying and thinking about all the good times my wife and I had had on Christmas. It came at me out of the blue. I cried for fifteen minutes and then I pulled myself together. It was weird. It had been nine months prior to that that I had had a similar emotional breakdown.

I was confused. What had happened? I talked to one of my divorce buddies about the whole thing. She smiled and told me that a similar thing had happened to her. Something about the holiday had just stirred up the emotions in both of us. That made me feel better.

This was just proof, that while I had moved on with my life, I still had an emotional scar. So did she. Maybe we all do when we get through an emotional experience as rough as a divorce.

I am not writing this to scare you. I am simply writing this, so, if you have a similar experience, you too will not feel alone. It's normal, and it's OK. It's just a scar.

Made in United States
North Haven, CT
07 December 2023

45137539R00071